Written by Pierre Pfeffer
Illustrated by René Mettler

Specialist adviser: Steve Pollock,
The British Museum
(Natural History)

ISBN 1 85103 023 9
First published 1987 in the United Kingdom by
Moonlight Publishing Ltd,
131 Kensington Church Street, London W8

Translated by Sarah Matthews

Printed in Italy by La Editoriale Libraria

The Long Life and Gentle Ways of the Elephant

How big is an elephant?

Elephants are the biggest animals that walk the earth. Did you know that an adult male can sometimes be as tall as the first storey of a house? Elephants are the heaviest of all land animals too: they can weigh as much as 100 grown-up people all weighed together! But all the same, elephants move about gently and quietly. They are very intelligent as well. With their size, their strength and their wisdom they walk the world without fear – who would dare attack them? Even a hunting lion moves out of their way. Elephants are vegetarians and harm no living creature, attacking others only when they feel threatened.

They live in Africa and Asia. The African elephant is bigger than the Indian elephant.

The moeritherium was the size of a pig, and had a long nose like a tapir.

Who was the elephant's ancestor?

The moeritherium, who lived in the swamps of Egypt over 60 million years ago. Slowly, generation by generation, its descendants grew bigger and bigger. Their noses gradually lengthened until they finally developed into a trunk which they used to pick up their food. Their upper teeth also grew and became tusks.

Have you seen pictures of mammoths? They were related to elephants, but had long hair and curly tusks. They first appeared on earth 10 million years ago.

Dinotherium

Mastodon

What are tusks for?

They can be used for fighting, for grubbing up roots, for digging down into damp sand to find drinking water. Other animals like giraffes and rhinoceros share the water the elephants find.

The African elephant has two lips at the end of its trunk.

Elephants often use one tusk rather than the other: they are right-tusked or left-tusked! Their tusks grow all their lives, and can be 3 metres long and weigh as much as 100 kilos each.

Elephants have big teeth, too, flat molars which they use to grind up the vegetation they eat. As these teeth wear down they are replaced – six times during the course of an elephant's life.

Elephants spend all day and most of the night feeding themselves.

In Asia, only male elephants have visible tusks.

They only sleep for 4 hours! A full-grown elephant eats 150 kilos of leaves, grass, fruit and roots every day. Sometimes, in order to reach the leaves, they'll uproot a whole tree! They have to drink a lot of water too: 70-90 litres a day!

Elephants are not all the same.

Indian elephants have smaller ears, a rounder head, and only one lip at the end of their trunks. Their tusks are shorter. Living in the dense, steamy tropical forests, they hardly ever gather into enormous herds as African elephants do.

What is a tool, a hand, a pump, a snorkel, a trumpet and a nose?

An elephant's trunk! It is hollow and boneless, made of muscle and ending in sensitive lips. Thanks to its trunk, an elephant can breathe, pick fruit, throw a lion into the air! It can use it to drink, and to shower itself with water – a great delight under the hot sun. If an elephant swims underwater, it can hold its trunk above the surface to breathe. It's a trumpet, too: when an elephant calls out you can hear it for miles around! And it lifts its trunk in the air to sniff out danger...

Did you know that elephants have very thin, sensitive skin?

Sharp grasses scratch them, tsetse flies and tics, a sort of tiny spider, bite them and suck their blood. To protect themselves, elephants roll in mud. As the mud dries, it cakes on into a sort of armour.

Sometimes elephants spray themselves with dust as well. A little bird, called a tic-bird, helps them by picking off the parasites and eating them.

If an elephant gets too hot, it will flap its huge ears, using them like a fan!

African elephants live in vast herds.

In every herd there are several family groups, made up of a mother and her children of all ages. The leader of the herd is an old female.

The adult males, especially the old ones, live apart in little groups of 2 or 3, or on their own.

In Africa, during the dry season, the elephants move towards the forests, where there are always leaves for them to eat and water for them to drink. Once the rains come, they move in their hundreds back onto the plains where the fresh green grass has begun to grow.
An elephant can easily walk 30 km in a day, swinging along on its big, thick-skinned feet.

Danger!

One elephant sounds the alarm, trumpeting loudly through its trunk. The others stop eating and squeeze up close together in a circle, with the babies in the middle. The old cow-elephant moves forward, ears flapping. If she sees an attacker, she charges, head down, tusks forward.

Elephants are very affectionate: they touch and stroke each other with their trunks, or push against each other, pretending to fight!

A baby elephant is born!

It weighs 120 kilos, and is covered in soft, reddish hair. It has been growing inside its mother for twenty-two months: nearly two years. An hour after it is born, the baby elephant can stand and suckle from its mother's nipples, which are between her front legs. The mother looks after the baby and protects it from danger. She helps it cross difficult ground by supporting it round the middle with her trunk. The baby feeds from its mother for about a year. At ten years old, it is an adult.

Elephants live to a great age.

They usually die of hunger when they're about 50 or 60 years old: their teeth have worn away and they can only eat soft plants from swamps and bogs.

It is against the law to kill elephants, but poachers hunt them for the ivory in their tusks, and farmers kill them if they harm their crops. Lions and tigers only attack babies and elephants that are ill. When elephants are ill or dying, other members of the group gather to help. They hold the sick elephant up and help it to move and feed. Even when an elephant has died, they try to help it stand up again.

Every elephant has its own keeper, or mahout, who will look after it all its life.

Helpful and strong

In India, people have used the strength and intelligence of elephants for a long time. The elephants help them with hard and heavy work. Young elephants are caught and trained with the help of elephants which have been trained already.

This elephant is lifting a tree-trunk in its trunk.

At elephant school,
elephants learn to understand some words and how to carry their mahouts. Later on an elephant will learn how to hold heavier and heavier tree-trunks. Once he has finished learning, he goes to work in the forest. Elephants can cross bogs where bulldozers get stuck.

Friends together!

Every day, the mahout takes his elephant down to the river for a good wash and brush-up. He even cleans the elephant's teeth with tree-bark. The mahout talks to the elephant or tugs its ears to tell it where to go.

An elephant never forgets.

An elephant can remember all the different commands given by its mahout. It can also recognise a great many friends, both elephants and people.

Where do elephants get dressed up?
In India and South-east Asia.

Once upon a time, kings and maharajas owned hundreds of elephants, with tusks painted red and gold. Nowadays elephants are at their grandest dressed in their finery for feast-days.

Famous elephants

In India, the god **Ganesh** is shown with an elephant's head. Ganesh has strength and wisdom. Schoolchildren and students pray to him before their exams.

Two thousand years ago, a general called Hannibal from Carthage in Africa wanted to attack the Romans. To surprise and frighten them, he led an **army of fighting elephants** into Italy over the Alps.

Another famous elephant is the gigantic **Ahmed**, who is classed as a national monument in Kenya! His stuffed body is in the museum in Nairobi.

Elephant records

The biggest elephant: 4 metres high.
The longest tusk: 3.5 metres.
The heaviest tusk: 130 kilos.

True or false?

1. Elephants are afraid of mice.
2. A baby elephant sucks its trunk.
3. There are elephant graveyards.
4. The hairs from an elephant's tail are used to make bracelets.

This elephant is digging in the ground to find water.

5. African elephants can't be trained.
6. Elephants sometimes walk along in a line, holding each other's tails.
7. You can tell how old an elephant is by looking at its teeth.
8. An elephant can run at 40 km an hour.

1. True. 2. True: it sucks its trunk just like a child sucking its thumb. 3. False: this myth grew up because sometimes whole herds die together, trapped in a swamp. 4. True. 5. False: but they are much harder to train than Indian elephants. 6. True. 7. True. 8. True, but not for very long.

Index